The Hairy-Scary Monster

Cynthia Rider • Alex Brychta

OXFORD
UNIVERSITY PRESS

Kipper didn't want to go to sleep.
"Biff and Chip are at Gran's," he
said. "I don't like being on my own."

"Poor Kipper," thought Floppy.
"I'll stay with him."

"Oh no, Floppy," said Mum.
"Kipper is going to sleep."

But Kipper wasn't going to sleep.
He was wide awake.
"I can't go to sleep," he grumbled.
"I just can't!"

Kipper laughed. "I know! I'll play a trick," he said. "I'll trick Dad and get him to come upstairs."

He jumped up and down on his bed. "Dad!" he yelled. "There's a hairy-scary monster! It's coming to get me, Dad. Help!"

Dad ran up to Kipper's bedroom.
Floppy barked and ran after him.
"What monster?" said Dad.
"Where is it?"

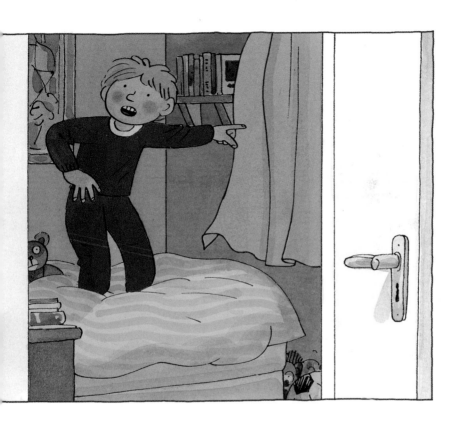

Kipper pointed to the curtains.
"It's behind the curtains," he said.
"It's got sharp yellow teeth and
glowing red eyes."

Dad looked behind the curtains,
but he didn't see a monster.

"There's no monster here," he
said. "Look!"

"It was a trick," laughed Kipper.
"It was just a trick!"

Dad laughed, and tucked Kipper
up. "Be a good boy and go to sleep,"
he said. "And no more tricks!"

Floppy was hiding. He didn't
like monsters.

"Come out, Floppy," said Dad.
"Kipper is going to sleep."

But Kipper wasn't going to sleep.
He was still wide awake.

"I don't like being on my own,"
he grumbled. "It's boring."

Kipper laughed. "I know! I'll play
another trick," he said. "I'll trick
Mum and get her to come upstairs."

"Mum!" yelled Kipper. "There's a
hairy-scary monster! It's going to
eat me up. Mum, help!"

Mum ran up to Kipper's bedroom.
Floppy barked and ran after her.

"What monster?" said Mum.
"Where is it?"

Kipper pointed to the wardrobe.
"It's in the wardrobe," he said.
"It's got long sharp claws and
hairy jaws."

Mum looked in the wardrobe, but
she didn't see a monster.

"There's no monster here," she
said. "Look!"

"It was a trick!" laughed Kipper.
"It was just a trick."

Mum tucked Kipper up again.
"Be a good boy and go to sleep,"
she said. "And no more tricks!"

Kipper began to fall asleep. His
eyes were just closing when he heard
something under the bed.

It was something that was snuffling.
It was something that was snorting. It
was something that was hairy and
very, very scary!

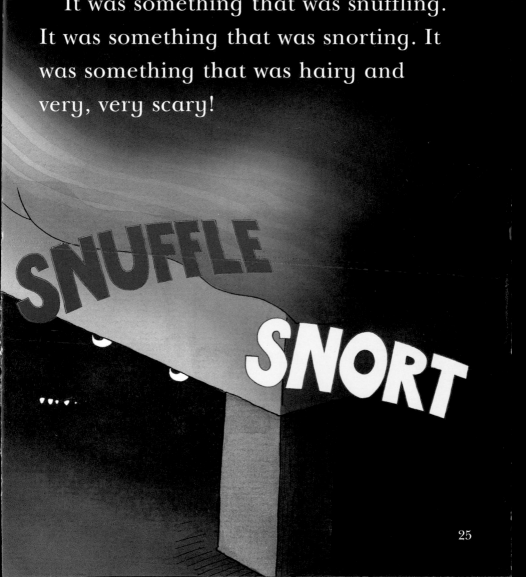

"Help!" yelled Kipper. "There really is a monster! Mum, Dad, help me! I'm scared!"

Mum and Dad ran upstairs.

"What's wrong, Kipper?" they said.

"There's a monster," he sobbed.

"There's a monster under the bed."

Dad looked under the bed.

"There is a monster!" he said. "It's the Hairy-Scary Floppy Monster!"

Think about the story

Why didn't Kipper want to go to sleep?

Which three places did Kipper say the monster was hiding?

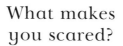

What things made you laugh in the story?

What makes you scared?

Hide and Seek

What is the monster hiding from? Find the words that rhyme. The words that are left tell you what the monster is hiding from.

claws

trick

hairy

man

mouse

little

pan

stick

jaws

scary

Useful common words repeated in this story and other books in the series. after behind being can't didn't don't help just know laughed more something there's under upstairs
Names in this story: Mum Dad Biff Chip Gran Kipper Floppy